# The Tactics of Pitching

*The Art, Science, and Strategy of Playing Baseball's Most Important Position*

# Branford McAllister

Copyright © 2013 Branford McAllister
All rights reserved.

ISBN: 1482624966
ISBN 13: 9781482624960

# THE TACTICS OF PITCHING:

## The Art, Science, and Strategy of Playing Baseball's Most Important Position

Branford McAllister

# TABLE OF CONTENTS

INTRODUCTION .................................................................. 3
PITCHING PHILOSOPHY ...................................................... 5
HOW AIR RESISTANCE AFFECTS THE FLIGHT OF A BALL ... 13
THE STRIKEZONE ............................................................... 17
PITCHES ............................................................................. 19
HOW DIFFERENT PITCHES ARE THROWN ........................... 27
SITUATIONAL PITCHING ..................................................... 39
WARMING UP TO PITCH A GAME ........................................ 55
CORRECTING PROBLEMS .................................................... 57
MENTAL ASPECTS OF PITCHING .......................................... 59
PITCHING MECHANICS:  A CHECKLIST ................................ 65
THE NINTH INNING:  THE FINISH ....................................... 71
ABOUT THE AUTHOR .......................................................... 73

# INTRODUCTION

I have played, coached, studied, and watched baseball for well over 50 years. My playing, as a pitcher, extended into college and bit beyond. I have coached amateur baseball and, specifically pitching, up to the high school level. And, I have talked to many college and pro players and coaches. Over the years, I have seen many books on baseball, a few of them about pitching. Most of them are concerned with mechanics, and a few good ones on conditioning. And, most of these are very good—written by very experienced, professional baseball people. In that same time, I have seen very few good books on the art of pitching—specifically, books dealing with how to throw specific pitches, why they do what they do, when to throw them, to what locations, and how to set up hitters. Few books describe the mental aspects of pitching. More apparent is the general lack of knowledge among coaches, at all levels, about how to pitch. Many know the basic mechanics, some can even make good corrections. But few have the ability to help pitchers "pitch" a good game. Few understand the subtleties of how to throw pitches and how to formulate game plans for pitching. The outcome is poor pitch selection and a failure on the hill.

As a result of my view that there is a lack of good information out there on some very specific subjects related to pitching, and to express the knowledge about the subject for which I have had a passion during my 50+ years of playing, pitching, studying, and coaching, I offer this book. I hope that it benefits others who both practice the craft of pitching and teach others.

Because of the volume of good works dealing with mechanics and conditioning, I will offer only simple guidelines here, and refer the reader to other scholarly texts, such as the following:

*Fit to Pitch*, by Tom House
*Nolan Ryan's Pitcher's Bible*, by Nolan Ryan and Tom House
*Pitching: The Keys to Excellence*, by Pat Jordan
*Play Better Baseball*, by Bob Cluck.

I will also rely heavily upon some sources covering the physics of pitching—the science half of the art and science of pitching. These include the following:

*The Physics of Baseball*, by Robert K. Adair

Finally, here are some sources that I find relevant and useful in the discussion:

The websites, www.fangraphs.com and www2.baseballinfosolutions.com, plus all their links
*Golf is Not a Game of Perfect*, by Dr. Bob Rotella (the mental aspects of golf, closely related to pitching); and, *The Golfer's Mind: Play to Play Great*, by Dr. Bob Rotella and Bob Cullen (similarly on the mental aspects of golf, and by extension, pitching)

What I will concentrate on are the following topics:

Pitching Philosophy
How Air Resistance Affects the Flight of a Ball
The Strikezone
Pitches
Situational Pitching
Mechanics Checklist
Correcting Problems
Mental Aspects of Pitching.

# PITCHING PHILOSOPHY

### HOW TO BEAT HITTERS—PITCHERS VERSUS THROWERS

There are two basic ways to win the pitcher versus hitter war:
1. Overpower the hitter (like Justin Verlander)
2. Fool the hitter (like Barry Zito).

The first requires dominating stuff, generally velocity. (According to www.fangraphs.com Verlander's average fastball in 2012 was 94.3 mph. He also showcased a superb curveball.) And, it requires a fair amount of control to go with the overpowering velocity. Not many pitchers have that kind of ability, even in the major leagues. For another thing, at each higher level, not only are the pitchers better, but so are the hitters. It is just tough to get fastballs by very good hitters every time they come up and on every pitch. At lower levels, very few pitchers have the kind of overpowering stuff to rely just on that to get hitters out throughout a game. Those who do have electric stuff can dominate low-level hitters. They are the fortunate ones, but not everyone has this advantage. For them, and for the overpowering pitchers at higher levels, something more than great stuff is required.

So, in general, the better strategy is #2—fool hitters. This requires some weapons besides a dominating fastball. (Barry Zito went 15-8 with the 2012 champion Giants with a fastball averaging 83.7 mph.)

Of course, if you possess overpowering stuff and great command, a combination of #1 and #2 is an almost unbeatable strategy. And, we have to think about sustaining our stuff over an entire season. We will discuss this a bit more later.

> 1. Batter takes a ball
> 2. Batter takes a strike
> 3. Batter swings and misses
>    - Ahead
>    - Behind
>    - Over
>    - Under
> 4. Contact but foul ⎫        ⎧ Off the end
> 5. Contact, weak ball on the ground ⎬ ⎨ Off the handle
> 6. Contact, weak ball in the air ⎪    ⎪ Over
> 7. Hit well ⎭                  ⎩ Under
>
> Table 1. Seven outcomes of pitched balls

## What is the Objective on the Mound?

What do we mean by fooling hitters? We mean here being a *pitcher* and not simply a *thrower*.

There are only a handful of possible outcomes from each pitched ball, shown in Table 1.

The objective is to (a) make the batter swing and miss (using some combination of movement, speed, and location); (b) get the batter to make a bad swing; or (3) cause the batter to make a bad decision (take a strike, chase a ball out of the zone).

Of the seven outcomes in Table 1, all but one are desirable. So, how hard can it be if six of the seven outcomes are favorable to the pitcher?

## Pitcher's Tools

What tools does a pitcher have at his disposal? On any given pitch, he can vary the speed of his pitches, hit various locations, and get movement.

He can use these tools in various combinations or sequences, as part of a *strategy* of pitching a game that achieves some *tactical advantage* over the hitter.

More precisely, there are seven specific effects the pitcher can control, shown in Table 2. We will discuss most of these in detail later. For now, let's continue the discussion on pitching philosophy.

- Pitching motion
- Release point in three-dimensional space
- Speed
- Direction (from release to strikezone)
- Spin (axis and rate)
- Seam orientation
- Sequence of pitches

Table 2. What pitchers can control

## WHAT IS DEMANDED OF A PITCHER TO BE SUCCESSFUL?

This approach (of being a *pitcher* and not a *thrower*) demands several attributes. Here are three:

1. **A few pitches.** Besides a fastball, a pitcher needs an off-speed pitch and a breaking ball. Doesn't matter what they are. Just one pitch slower than a fastball delivered with a motion that looks like a fastball. And one that moves in a direction different from a fastball (preferably down).

2. **Control.** The ideal goal is to be able to hit the target with any pitch at any time. Consistent control comes from a predictable and consistent release point, which in turn results from consistent and sound mechanics during the windup and delivery. The sound mechanics enable a pitcher to sustain control over a game, which one might call *command*.

Let's briefly touch on the distinction between these two concepts: *control* and *command*. There are various explanations of the difference out there, but here are two.

The first describes *control* as the ability to throw any given pitch consistently to the desired location, within a reasonable amount of variation or error. In contrast, *command* would indicate the consistent ability to control all pitches in the arsenal over the course of an outing.

The second description says that *control* over one's pitches means that a pitcher is able to throw consistently to the strikezone. Most believe that a pitcher needs to have the ability to throw a fastball for a strike at any time during an at-bat. And, he needs his breaking balls or offspeed pitches to cross the plate in the strikezone. Generally, if a pitcher is routinely recording quick outs and getting ahead of hitters, then we would consider that he has good control because he is routinely throwing strikes.

On the other hand, *command* is a logical extension or refinement of control. Once a pitcher gains control over his pitches, then he must move on to learning command. Pitchers with good command have the capability to place their pitches any where they want within the strikezone (or, more to the point, at a desired target); they are able to throw not just strikes, but *good strikes*—those that create one of the favorable outcomes listed in Table 1, especially swings and misses, but we might include outcomes 2 through 6 here.

Now, one might then logically point out that command means more than just consistently throwing good strikes. Rather, command implies the capability of throwing consistently to the desired target, whether or not that is in the strikezone. So, we are really not talking simply about good strikes, but good pitches. We are talking about *hitting spots* not just throwing strikes.

And this gets us to the third attribute of a successful pitcher, the game plan (strategy).

3. **Some kind of strategy.** This is our game plan which includes an approach to facing the opponent's lineup, and more than once through. This I would call the *game strategy*. The strategy also includes what I call the *tactics of pitching*—the sequence of pitches to a hitter in any single at-bat. Let's consider the latter.

The first important part of our *tactics* is to get ahead in the count. It is often said that the best pitch you have is *strike one*. That doesn't mean piping a fastball every time. It does mean getting a strike somehow. The better your control, the more options you have. If you can hit the target consistently with every pitch, then you can get a strike with something other than a fastball, somewhere other than down the middle. And, this lessens the chance that an aggressive hitter tees off on the first pitch.

The second component in winning the *tactical battle* is to throw the right pitch, at the right spot, and the right time (remember the concept of *command?*). The right pitch in the wrong spot will not work (great fastball, thigh high, down the middle with an 0-2 count; this might have been great 2" off the outside corner at the knees). A great pitch at the wrong time won't hack it, either (changeup against a #8 hitter who can't hit the fastball). So, what that means is there needs to be a plan for getting hitters out—one that accounts for the hitter, the score, the inning, which at-bat this is for the hitter, how we pitched him previously, what we know from scouting the hitter, what is working, how we feel, and so on. **THIS IS THE MOST CHALLENGING PART OF THE GAME.**

So, this approach—pitching, not simply throwing to overpower the hitter—is the most successful for most. Many, if not most major league pitchers have what we would consider overpowering stuff. Some minor league and college pitchers do, too. Few high school pitchers do. But let's not forget the 2012 World Series. Justin Verlander has great stuff even on an off day. But, the Giants were able to get to him in spite of his stuff. It happens. Good hitters can catch up to any fastball. So, a combination of overpowering stuff, command, and strategy will lead to success at any level. But, at lower levels, even with average stuff, you can succeed with a combination of command and strategy.

## What Must a Pitcher Do to Succeed?

What makes all of this possible? It does not require a 90 mph fastball. Greg Maddux (four consecutive Cy Young awards) had a mid-80s fastball. It does not require a great curveball. What you need is to practice, have discipline, gain confidence, have a good catcher, plan well, think out there on the hill, and be tough.

Practicing (drills, live throwing) with good mechanics leads to consistency in the windup and delivery. This leads to consistent release points. This leads to command—consistently hitting spots. Any pitcher who has average stuff but can spot every pitch can win at the high school level—guaranteed—and probably higher.

Discipline means sticking to the game plan. Sometimes hitters get lucky and hit the right pitch thrown at the right spot at the wrong time. That probably means it wasn't the right pitch at the right spot at the right time. But, stuff happens. Sometimes, good hitters hit good pitches in good spots. So, don't panic. Generally, if you think about the hitters, the situation, and what you did last time, you'll win if you have command.

Discipline also means doing all those things that make you ready to pitch in a game: get in shape, practice, warm up properly, study the hitters. Maddux spent hours studying hitters. That's one reason why he won. Nolan Ryan rode an exercise cycle for an hour after pitching in a night game.

Confidence has a funny quality. It comes from having some success, generally through solid practice. And, in turn, once you have some confidence, you find you can do what you want. It is a matter of the power of positive thinking—having a positive image in your mind's eye that is translated into a physical reproduction on the mound. A positive mental image will result in a good pitch. Confidence is the key. The wrong pitch with a confident mindset is better than the right pitch with doubt. Trust in your stuff.

A good catcher and a good pitching coach—especially whoever is calling pitches—is obviously a huge advantage. Pitchers often have no control over these factors. Do your best!

And, knowledge. There is no substitute for understanding your craft. How to throw pitches. Having a good feel for grips and the ball. Understanding your own mechanics and how to correct problems that arise during the game. Knowing when to throw what and where. Knowing the hitters. You can't have a good strategy on the mound if that strategy is based on things you haven't taken the time to learn. That is the purpose here. We will elaborate on these considerations later.

Finally, you have to be tough. It will almost never go perfectly. There will be errors, bad hops, bad calls, bad pitches. But, you have zero control over the last pitch. So, bear down and worry about the next pitch. Don't let the last pitch affect the rest. More games are lost because the pitcher lost his composure and concentration than because he lost his stuff. Relax, rely on your muscle memory gained through hard work in practice, and get the next guy by hitting the glove with the pitch called. And, never let them see you sweat. Be tougher than anyone else on that field.

## THE FINAL WORD ON PHILOSOPHY

Most of us weren't born with Justin Verlander's arm. We all could improve our velocity with better mechanics and strength training. But, most of us will not overpower every hitter every at bat. So, we have to rely on skill and cunning—making hitters make mistakes. Making them hit pitches where they have little chance of success. Making them chase balls out of the strikezone. And that comes from getting ahead in the count by throwing good pitches for strikes, then forcing the hitter to protect the plate against marginal strikes. That requires practice, discipline, and mental preparation. It's really simple. Just takes some hard work.

We now turn to the tools of the trade—how to apply the philosophy in practical terms.

# HOW AIR RESISTANCE AFFECTS THE FLIGHT OF A BALL

At the typical velocities baseballs travel, air resistance is surprisingly lower for the turbulent flow that results from the raised stitches (seams) than it would be for a smooth ball of the same dimensions (without seams). This is important when we talk about 4-seam versus 2-seam pitches. The seams induce a low-resistance turbulent air flow, making it sustain its velocity longer than a smoother ball. A stitched ball that would normally travel 400 feet would travel only 300 feet if it were smooth.

The drag on a rotating baseball, and hence the effect on its velocity and movement, depends on the following:

1. The axis of rotation with respect to the seams (orientation of the seams).
2. The orientation of the axis of rotation with respect to the ground.
3. The rate of the rotation (how fast it is spinning).

Generally, atmospheric pressure exerts an equal force on all sides of a ball traveling toward the plate. However, if the forces on one side of ball differ, even by just a small amount, the flight path of the ball can be altered—curved—by a noticeable amount. Such asymmetrical force imbalances are generated by either spin or the asymmetric placement of the stitches in the windstream. See Figure 1.

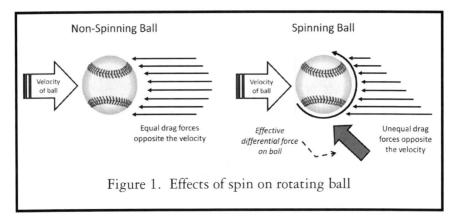

Figure 1. Effects of spin on rotating ball

A spinning ball is characterized by different effective wind velocities—airspeed—on either side of the ball. The velocity through the air on one side of the ball is greater than the air velocity on the other side of the ball. This results in a greater force applied on the faster side of the ball than the slower side. This differential force causes the ball to be deflected toward the slower spinning side along its normally straight flight path toward the plate.

The greater the spin, the greater the differential between air velocities on opposite sides of the ball. Thus, the greater the spin, the greater the deflection from a straight flight path (more break).

For a given spin rate, the effect of the differential forces on the ball due to spin is greatest at about 60 mph. Thus, for the same amount of spin, the greatest break will be realized at 60 mph. The faster the pitch above 60, the less the break with the same spin rate. Additionally, the differential forces on the ball due to spin have less and less time to act upon the flight of the ball the greater the velocity above 60.

Other forces affecting the deceleration of the ball in flight are wind and air density.

Density is affected by altitude (less dense at higher elevations), temperature (hotter = less density), barometric pressure (lower pressure = less density), and humidity.

Humidity, by itself, has very little effect on the flight of the ball. Interestingly, and contrary to popular wisdom, in greater humidity, the ball will decelerate less—have a higher velocity—travel farther—because water vapor is a little lighter than air. Humidity can, however, affect the weight and elasticity of balls in storage—higher humidity makes the ball predictably heavier and less elastic (less trampoline effect off a bat).

So, average velocity is increased at higher altitudes, on hot and humid days, with low barometric pressure (i.e., those conditions where the air is less dense).

In contrast, the effectiveness of spin behaves in the opposite direction. Spin is more effective at low altitudes, on colder or drier days, with high pressure. That assumes you can generate the same amount of spin, especially tough when the weather is cold.

At Coors Field, in Denver, on a hot summer day, the pitcher can expect to have greater velocity and less movement, than at Jacobs Field in Cleveland on a late fall day with cold temperatures.

Wind in the face of the pitcher lowers the average velocity through the pitch time of flight, but results in considerably more movement. With a wind at the pitcher's back, he can expect greater velocity and less movement. The other obvious effect is the carry of a batted ball with the wind blowing in or out.

One other factor is the quality of individual balls. Interestingly, a scuffed up ball—a rougher surface than a new ball—may actually have less drag as the result of a more uniform turbulent airflow over the surface of the ball, and therefore travel faster and farther than a new ball. The difference in the height of the seams has a negligible effect on the flight of the ball. However, both factors—roughness and seams—affect how well the pitcher can grip the ball.

Finally, a thrown ball decelerates due to air resistance (drag) approximately 7 mph during its time of flight from release to crossing the front of the plate.

These are all things that explain why pitched balls do what they do. Some of these are things that the pitcher needs to consider in preparing for a ballgame.

# THE STRIKEZONE

A strike is, or should be, called whenever any part of the ball passes through any part of the strikezone. The strikezone is the space over home plate between the batter's armpits and the top of his knees when he assumes a natural stance.

A typical 6' tall batter stands naturally at the plate with his armpits 46" above the plate. The tops of his knees will be about 22" above the plate. As a matter of practice, umpires define the high boundary of the strikezone about 4" lower than the armpits. So, the effective zone is about 20" in height (from 22" above the plate to 42").

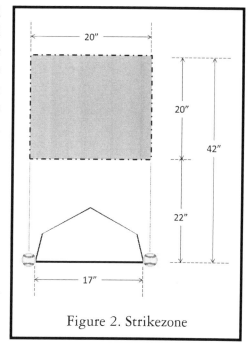

Figure 2. Strikezone

Home plate is 17 inches wide. Since any part of the ball must pass over the plate to be a strike, the center of the ball (about 3" in diameter) must pass within a zone 20" wide.

Thus, the effective strikezone is 20x20, as shown in Figure 2.

In order to prevent the batter from making contact, or at best making only partial contact, the pitcher varies the pitch to pass through specific parts of the strikezone (or out of it), at different velocities (changing speeds to upset the batter's timing), or by applying varying spins—amount and axis—to change the movement of the ball.

The pitcher's action up to the release of the ball is the art of pitching—location, velocity, and movement—and the factors affecting the ball once released are determined by physics—the laws of nature.

As we said earlier, the difference in air resistance around a spinning ball causes a difference in the forces acting on either side. That, in turn, causes the ball to move on a curved path.

We will now discuss the various pitches used to vary location, velocity, and movement. Then, we'll talk about how and where those pitches are thrown. And finally, we'll discuss how to set up hitters in order to fool them.

# PITCHES

Different pitches are characterized by the direction of their spin, and the axis about which the ball rotates. These are illustrated in Figure 3. In this section, we are talking only about the characteristics of each pitch (spin and trajectory), not how to throw them. We'll cover that in the next section.

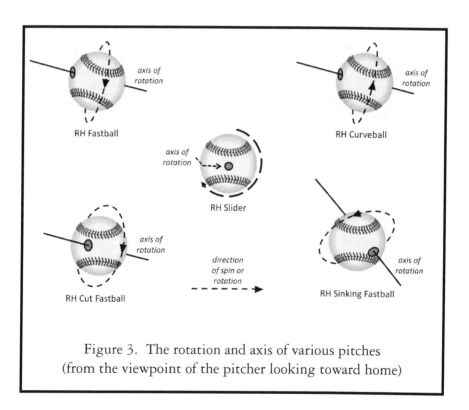

Figure 3. The rotation and axis of various pitches
(from the viewpoint of the pitcher looking toward home)

Figure 4 shows the notional trajectories of several pitches. The assumptions are: a 6' tall pitcher on a 10" mound releases the ball approximately 6' above the level of the infield and about 6' in front of the rubber.

Three primary forces act on the ball after it has been thrown:

1. Air resistance. This force slows the ball during its time of flight. The magnitude of this deceleration is approximately 7 mph from release to the front of the plate. Thus, an 87 mph fastball reaches the front of the plate at 80 mph.

2. Gravity. A ball with an average velocity of 85 mph and with little or no spin would fall approximately 3 feet during the average time of flight from release to the front of the plate. Thus, a ball thrown level at 88 mph, 6 feet above the infield, would arrive at the plate 3 feet, or 36 inches high, at 81 mph. This is illustrated in trajectory number 2 in Figure 4. (A major league fastball averaging 90 mph for a time of flight of roughly 0.4 seconds would drop 32" due to gravity.) In addition, this ball will drop approximately an additional 4" in the 3 feet it travels from the front of the plate to the catcher's glove.

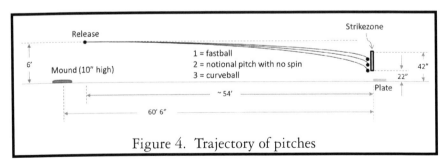

Figure 4. Trajectory of pitches

In actuality, the pitcher may choose to aim lower so that the ball crosses the front of the plate at the bottom of the strikezone, 22" above the plate. Thus, the initial trajectory of a typical fastball is angled downward. Without considering spin (covered below), it drops over 3 feet.

3. Asymmetrical force on either side of the ball due to spin. This is due to the greater air resistance on the side of the ball spinning into the windstream compared to the other side of the ball, deflecting the ball in the direction of spin. Figure 4 shows this effect on the trajectory of a fastball (trajectory 1) and curveball (trajectory 3). More on this, and how it affects the actual trajectory of the pitch, below.

Figure 5 illustrates the deflection of a ball thrown with purely horizontal spin—a perfectly flat or sidearm curveball. The spin and axis are shown in Figure 6. If thrown initially at the left side of the plate (inside corner to a lefthanded batter), at 70 mph, spinning at 1600 rpm, the pitch moves 14.4 inches from left to right.

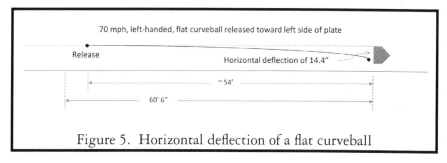

Figure 5. Horizontal deflection of a flat curveball

From a practical standpoint, such a purely horizontal movement is only theoretical. However, data from www.fangraphs.com provide empirical evidence about the horizontal movement of major league pitches. In 2012, the largest average horizontal movement was roughly 13".

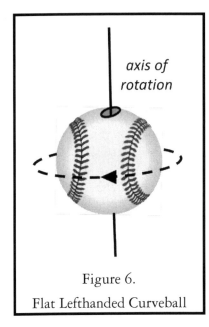

Figure 6.
Flat Lefthanded Curveball

Even more interesting is the fact that one half of the movement occurs during the last 15 feet of the pitch. This is due to the effects of the spin and the differential forces applied to the ball as it spins toward the plate. This is what gives the appearance of breaking late in the flight path of the pitch ("late break" or "late movement").

Of course, a pitch with less spin or more velocity, or whose spin axis is not purely vertical, will not break as much in the horizontal. As the spin axis is rotated from vertical toward horizontal (from a sidearm curveball to more overhand), the plane of the break is moved more downward. The typical curveball has a component of movement in both the horizontal and the vertical.

Thus, if the spin of a curveball is oriented downward, a pitch released on a vector parallel to the ground will drop 3 feet due to gravity plus another 14 inches or so, for a total of about 4 feet. That is, it will begin at release at 6 feet and cross the front of the plate at 24 inches—just inside the strikezone. It will continue to drop so that the catcher will receive the ball just above the ground. Some of the best curveballs actually hit the dirt just prior to being caught. They may be in or just below the strikezone. However, they appear to be high enough to be strikes when still enroute to the plate, especially if the batter does not recognize the spin, or mistakes the downward spin for the backspin typical of a fastball. So, the curveball not only is slower than a fastball—causing the batter difficulty because of the change of speed—but looks like a strike until late in the flight path—"late break."

Also, pitches whose axis is neither perfectly vertical or horizontal will break less. Examples include sliders and cut fastballs, generally thrown with more velocity and less strictly downward or side spin. Refer back to Figure 3.

A well thrown, purely overhand fastball, with backspin (see Figure 3), has the effect of "hopping" or rising—according to www.fangraphs.com, between 2" and 12" for a major league pitcher (excluding gravity), with half of that movement occurring in the last 15 feet before crossing the plate. In other words, in the absence of gravity, a major league fastball would rise as much as a foot. The key is, this movement is away from the falling arc on the ball due to gravity. Thus, whereas a ball would drop about 3 feet due to gravity, the overhand fastball moves upward from this arc about 4 inches nominally, as illustrated in trajectory 1 of Figure 4. Again, it is the backspin that causes the ball to be deflected upward from the expected flight path with only gravity affecting it. The flight of the ball is not really rising, but has the appearance of rising because we become accustomed to a trajectory and assume it to be straight.

A fastball thrown other than overhand—¾ or sidearm—has a spin axis rotated clockwise. The movement due to spin is therefore not vertical, but a combination of up and to the right (for a righthanded pitcher). See Figure 7. Therefore, the spin does not counteract gravity drop as much. So, the pitch drops more and we typically interpret this as "sinking." This is because it drops more than we expect.

Now, let's consider off-speed pitches, including curveballs and changeups. These start slower, and perhaps decelerate more, than a fastball. Thus, with lower average speed, and a greater time inflight, we would expect a larger drop due to gravity. So, in general, slower pitches are airborne longer and drop more due to gravity. And, therefore, this difference in gravity drop makes us believe that the fastball "rises" and the other pitches "drop."

Another consideration is the pitcher's grip on the seams. The 2-seam fastball, has a smoother aerodynamic profile in the air because only 2 seams are presented perpendicular to the windstream, and therefore more drag than a 4-seam fastball. The 4-seam fastball is less smooth and therefore has less drag. It is

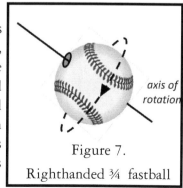

Figure 7.
Righthanded ¾ fastball

possible that the velocities crossing the front of the plate can differ by as much as 4 mph between the 4-seam (faster) and the 2-seam.

In terms of movement, the pitch that generated less drag (the 4-seamer) would also generate less differential force due to spin (less movement) than the 2-seamer. Thus, the 4-seam fastball generally has greater velocity and less movement than the 2-seamer.

## Specialty Pitches

The knuckleball is characterized by little or no spin. The three main forces still act on the ball—air resistance, gravity, and differential pressures. Gravity causes the ball to drop, and air resistance slows the ball down in flight. However, because of its lack of spin, and the irregular configuration of the stitches in the windstream, the differential air pressures all around the ball are random, irregular, and unpredictable. So, the pitch tends to float in odd directions, making it tough to catch and even more difficult to hit. If any spin is introduced inadvertently, then the air pressures tend to become more conventional and predictable—similar to any other normal pitch—but without the amount of movement and at much lower velocity. Thus, a knuckleball that doesn't "knuckle"—has some spin—is easy to hit.

The split-fingered fastball is thrown with the fingers spread apart. This has two effects: (a) less velocity; and, (b) a decreased amount of backspin normally achieved with a conventional fastball, while maintaining some velocity—less than the fastball but more than a change or curveball. The lack of spin—usually resulting in a tumbling ball—does not hop the 4 inches upward. Rather, it falls due to gravity plus any additional downward movement due to any downward spin. So, it may appear to the batter as a fastball—due to the pitcher's arm motion and the speed of the pitch—but tends to "sink" as opposed to "rising" like a fastball. A splitter can reach the plate as much as 16 inches lower than a fastball that begins on the same trajectory. And, with its lower speed, it can fool the batter in two ways. Lower speed, longer time of flight, more gravity drop—all with the arm speed of a fastball.

The identifying characteristic of the slider is the clock-wise spin around the axis along the flight path of the ball toward the plate. This is seen as a "dot"—the center of the spin of a properly thrown slider as seen by either the pitcher, catcher, or batter. It is thrown hard (slower that a fastball, faster than a curveball, closer in velocity to the fastball). The slider looks like a fastball, except for its characteristic "dot," because of the arm movement and velocity. It tends to break several inches away from a right-handed batter and, depending on velocity, downward. Again, it is slower because the fingers are not applying the full force of the arm through the center of the ball, but rather offset to the side. So, we impart a different spin from a fastball (see Figure 3), with less velocity and more gravity drop.

The cut fastball or cutter is characterized by a spin axis somewhere between a fastball and a slider. Therefore, the spin around the axis between the pitcher and the batter is not so pronounced. It is thrown faster than the slider, but slightly slower than the fastball (but not much). For a righthanded pitcher, there is some movement away from a right-handed hitter.

A sinking fastball or "sinker" is nothing more than a fastball thrown with flatter spin, either as the result of a lower arm angle (¾ or sidearm) or finger pressure (see Figure 3). The spin axis can be either perpendicular to the ground (flat spin into the right-handed batter) or rotated slightly upward depending on grip and release. The pitch moves into the right-handed batter and generally drops more than a fastball (why it came to be called a sinker), due to less velocity and greater gravity drop.

The "slurve" is a cross between a curveball and a slider. The spin is flatter than an overhand curveball, but the spin axis is not rotated around as far as the slider. There may be the characteristic slider dot, but it will be displaced on the ball away from the right-handed batter, as he and the catcher would see it. It is thrown with roughly the velocity range between a curveball and a slider. The break is flatter than the curveball and bigger than the slider. This is the most common breaking ball because it is easier to throw than a curveball that breaks predominantly downward, but still effective because of the amount that it breaks, the fact that it breaks away from a right-handed hitter, and its change of speed off the fastball.

The truth of the matter is that breaking balls follow a spectrum, depending on the axis of spin, initial speed, and spin rate. So, these factors influence time of flight, horizontal movement, and vertical movement. Thus, we see, for example, a progression from fastball to cutter, to slider, to slurve, to curveball—with decreasing speed, greater horizontal movement, and greater vertical movement (drop or sink) along this continuum.

# HOW DIFFERENT PITCHES ARE THROWN

Having discussed spin and movement, we now look at how the pitcher delivers each pitch. We consider grip, pressure, motion, stride, and release. After that, we will discuss situations—when to throw each pitch, and to what location. Refer to Table 3 for a summary of the most common pitches.

| PITCH | SPIN (viewed by pitcher) | MOVEMENT (*) | SPEED | GRIP | RELEASE |
|---|---|---|---|---|---|
| Fastball: 4-seam | | ↗ | highest | • fingers close<br>• across wide 2 seams | even pressure on both fingers |
| Fastball: 2-seam | | ↗ | high (< 4-seam) | • fingers close<br>• on top of 2 seams or<br>• across narrow 2 seams | even pressure on both fingers |
| Sinker | | ↘ | above average | 2-seam grip | more pressure on index finger |
| Cutter | | ← | above average | 2-seam grip | more pressure on middle finger |
| Slider | | ← | above average | • fingers close<br>• middle finger along inside of long seam<br>• fingers on right side of ball | pressure on middle finger on side of ball to create clock-wise spin |
| Slurve | | ← | average | • fingers close<br>• middle finger along inside of long seam<br>• fingers on right side of ball | combination of slider and curve grip and spin |
| Curveball | | ↓ | below average | • fingers close<br>• middle finger along inside of long seam | pressure on middle finger on front of ball to create downspin |
| Changeup ("circle change") | | ↘ | slow | • form circle with thumb and index finger<br>• ball is deep in hand | ball released to outside of 3 fingers on ball |
| Splitter | tumbles | ↓ | above average | ball is between index and middle finger | ball tumbles out of fingers with no backspin and slight forward spin |

Table 3. Summary of pitches (* Movement is from normal, no-spin flight path affected only by gravity)

## FASTBALL

The fastball can be thrown in two basic ways: with two seams and with four (see Figures 8, 9, and 10). In either case, the index and middle fingers are place relatively close together, with the thumb underneath and slightly to the inside of the ball. The ball is relatively far out toward the finger tips. In fact, one comfortable position for the 4-seamer is for the top seam to cross just

Figure 8. 4-Seam fastball

below the last knuckle on each finger. The ball should be thrown with the same pressure on each finger, to ensure the maximum backspin—that is, so that the ball is spinning with an axis parallel to the ground and perpendicular to the flight of the ball. This also ensures the maximum finger pressure through the center of the ball, translating every body movement that precedes release into the maximum force applied to the ball—hence, maximum velocity. Any off-center pressure will decrease velocity and change the spin axis, and result in a cut fastball (pressure to the outside) or weak sinker (pressure on inside). These movements may be desirable for a purposeful cutter or sinker. However, when max velocity is desired, pressure must be through the center of the ball. This can be checked by watching the spin on the ball. Motion, stride, and release are the "baseline" mechanics for that pitcher. Anything else is a modification of these basic mechanics, for specific purposes.

The 2-seamer can be thrown with either the fingers across the narrow part of two seams (Figure 9) or with the seams (Figure 10).

The distinctions between the 2-seam and 4-seam fastballs are in velocity and movement. Generally, the 4-seamer

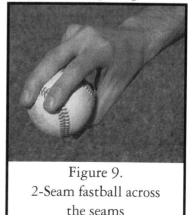

Figure 9.
2-Seam fastball across the seams

is faster (less drag on the ball due to uniform resistance from the four equally spaced seams rotating in the air stream). The 2-seamer will generally move more, depending on the release.

The 2-seamer moves as the result of two phenomena. The first is the tendency for the seams to cause the ball to sail, sometimes in unpredictable ways. This generally occurs with a new ball, which has high seams and a smooth texture. If thrown overhand, the ball may sail away from a right-handed hitter. Thrown ¾, the ball may sail into the hitter. The second way a 2-seamer moves is by altering the spin axis through subtle pressure on one finger or another. By applying added pressure on the middle finger, the pitch becomes more of a cut fastball, moving away from a right-handed hitter. With pressure on the index finger, the pitch moves into a right-handed hitter. The tradeoffs are in velocity, control, and movement. For example, the more the pitch resembles a cutter, the more it moves but the less velocity it has. But, slight pressure can create small movement and be difficult for the batter to detect.

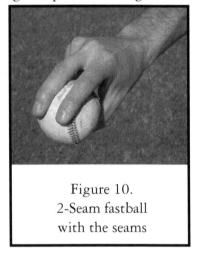

Figure 10.
2-Seam fastball
with the seams

In general, if you want to maximize velocity and control, throw the 4-seamer. For more movement, especially ahead in the count, throw the 2-seamer.

Obviously, the fastball can be thrown to any location depending on situation. In general, the best spots are down-and-in and down-and-away (any count). Ahead in the count, especially with two strikes, away outside the strikezone and up-and-in are effective. With good velocity, just high in the strikezone can be effective.

## Sinker

The most effective sinker is thrown with a motion between ¾ and sidearm, so that the spin is relatively flat compared to the conventional fastball. Movement can be maximized by using a 2-seam grip, and applying pressure on the index finger. The closer to sidearm, the greater the movement into a right-handed batter and down. When thrown overhand, the ball will not sink much. But, the pitcher can get some movement into the right-handed hitter, away from a left-handed hitter, by combining pressure on the index finger with some pronation during the release. That is, the pitcher can turn the ball over slightly (something like a screwball release, opposite the curveball or slider release). This has the additional effect of taking some velocity off the fastball—changing speeds and getting some movement. Motion and stride for a sinker are generally the same as the fastball.

A sinking fastball can also be effective by staying on top (versus dropping down more sidearm), and by applying subtle finger pressure to alter the axis of rotation slightly. The angle achieved by maintaining a high delivery (pitching "downhill"), and directing the pitch downward with a bit of side movement can yield a very effective sinker.

The sinker is effective almost exclusively down in the zone. It can start off in the strikezone, and break low. Best spots are inside to a right-hander, or a back-door sinker to catch the outside corner, if properly set up. Similarly, it can be a great pitch away to a left-handed batter.

## Cut Fastball

The cut fastball is thrown using the 2-seam grip with pressure applied to the middle finger. The greater the pressure, the more the spin changes from a fastball (backspin) toward a slider (clockwise spin). And, the greater the movement and the lower the velocity. Again, motion and stride are the same as the fastball.

The best location for the cutter is away to a right-hander or in on the fists of a left-handed hitter.

## CURVEBALL

The curveball is thrown by curling the fingers around the front of the ball, then pulling down the front of the ball to obtain downspin. The axis of the spin ranges from nearly straight down (thrown overhand) to relatively flat (sidearm). The basic grip (Figure 11) is to lay the middle finger along a seam, so that you can maximize the pressure along the right side of the finger applied to a seam (maximizing spin). It is not really important how the seams are

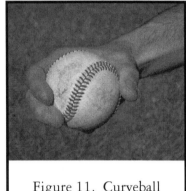

Figure 11. Curveball

aligned. Using the theory that more movement is achieved with two seams alignment (irregular drag pattern in the air flow), then ideally the spin should be applied like a 2-seam fastball, only in the opposite direction.

The motion should be as close to the fastball motion as possible. In other words, the arm motion should be difficult for the batter to differentiate from a fastball. If the pitcher throws a ¾ fastball, the curveball should be thrown ¾. Arm speed should be as fast as possible without compromising control.

Several theories are offered for stride. One theory states that the stride should be the same length as the fastball, for consistency. A second theory has the pitcher shortening the stride to get a bit more "over-the-top" body movement, especially for an overhand curveball, and therefore more downward leverage and spin. The danger with this method is the occasional tendency to leave the pitch high, due to an incomplete "finish." Or, that the pitcher overcompensates and throws the pitch into the dirt. A final theory has the pitcher lengthening the stride. This tends to bring the pitch down in the strikezone, where it is more effective. The disadvantage is the slight decrease in velocity and spin, so that if released high, it tends to hang. In practice, since curveballs are "feel" pitches rather than power pitches for most, some experimentation is needed to get into a groove. Depending on results, the pitcher can adjust release point and stride to achieve consistency.

Release is, as pointed out, a matter of feel. Several thought keys can be helpful. The pitcher can use a curveball grip—fingers together, middle finger along a seam, fingers curved around the front of the ball—and then thrown just like a fastball. This minimizes the number of "changes" from the fastball, while using the same motion. Another key is to imagine pulling the ball down in front of the pitcher—toward the catcher—with the pressure on the outside of the middle finger for a release out in front.

Several other mechanics must be stressed. It is important not to try to achieve curveball spin by rotating the wrist or elbow. Rather, the spin is achieved by pulling down on the middle finger across the front of the ball using a motion quite similar to a fastball.

Another important key is to avoid the tendency to open up too early with the left shoulder. This results in a flatter curveball that flies outside to a right-handed batter. The correction is to point the chin and left shoulder toward the catcher, down the stride line, for as long as possible.

The only place to throw a curveball is down in the zone—often below the strikezone where the catcher actually catches it in or near the dirt. It is most effective away from the hitter. Good hitters can generally handle the pitch if thrown inside. If flat, it can be effective beginning inside, but only rarely. Against left-handed hitters, it is most effective thrown away.

## SLIDER

The slider grip is similar to a curveball—fingers together, middle finger along a seam (Figure 12). However, the release is significantly different from a fastball and curveball. Instead, the slider is released with the fingers essentially pointed down the flight path of the ball, toward the catcher. The spin is obtained by pulling down on the right side of the ball, so that the ball has clock-wise spin around an axis between the pitcher and the catcher. Most of the

Figure 12. Slider

pressure is obtained with the outside of the middle finger. The ball is thrown hard, with arm motion as close to the fastball as possible. This, again, disguises the pitch, getting as much velocity as possible. The ball will be naturally slower than a fastball merely because the fingers are along the side of the ball, instead of through its center. Stride can be the same as the fastball.

A couple of cautions should be made about the slider. One is the tendency to drop the arm down to get more movement. This tips off the pitch, reduces velocity, and results in more of a ¾ "slurve." The desire is to throw a pitch with high velocity, tight spin, and small but rapid movement away from a right-handed hitter and down.

Another caution is to watch snapping off the pitch from the elbow while trying to get more spin. Snapping it off equates to really high arm speed with very rapid deceleration at or just after release. This is very damaging to the arm, particularly the elbow. A better approach is to stress a complete and smooth follow-through. Get velocity and spin by arm speed, not snap.

The slider is almost always most effective thrown down and away to a right-handed hitter, or into and down to a left handed hitter. It can be used to sneak in a back-door strike on the outside corner to a left-hander.

## CHANGE-UP

A change-up is any pitch that is thrown slower than a fastball. In other words, the idea is to fool the batter by making it look fastball (in motion and spin), only with less velocity and more movement. There are several ways to achieve this. One way is merely to take something off the fastball, to obtain a few miles per hour difference from the fastball. This can be very effective, especially since the motion can be roughly the same, and the release and spin are the same as the fastball, making it tough for the batter to pick up the speed difference. However, when the arm motion slows so much that the batter can detect it, then it loses its effectiveness as a change.

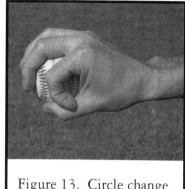

Figure 13. Circle change

So, one form of a changeup is simply to subtly take velocity off of a fastball—"change speeds"—in small amounts to get the batter just ahead of the pitch. This change of speeds will be discussed in a bit more detail later. Suffice to say, a simple difference in velocity changes the position of the ball for the same time of flight by feet: for example, a 5 mph difference results in a 3' difference in distance traveled for the time it takes from release to the front of the plate. A batter not adjusting will be 3' out front of the pitch.

Another way to achieve this is to alter the grip, so that the body movement is not translated directly through the center of the ball, and the ball travels at a slower velocity even though the motion looks the same as a fastball. A good way of doing this is the "circle change." Here, the pitcher forms a circle with the thumb and index finger, placing this circle on the inside of the ball (see Figure 13). The specifics can vary, with the index finger curling inside the thumb more or less depending on feel. The other three fingers are placed on top of the ball, again adjusted for feel and desired release and spin.

The desire is for the arm motion to be the same as a fastball, and for the ball to come out of the hand slower and with less backspin, or an altered spin axis, when compared to a fastball. Because the strongest two fingers are not on top of the ball (as with a fastball), and the ball is coming out of the grip to the side, the velocity is considerably reduced. Additionally, the spin, when most effective, is side spin—almost like a sinker. This can be enhanced if the pitcher pronates slightly—rotates the hand counterclockwise slightly—to achieve a bit of a "screwball" spin.

The end result is a slower pitch that moves right and down, even though it looks at release like a fastball. Because the grip achieves the slower velocity and spin, the arm movement can be just like a fastball, making it simple to throw. In this case, the only challenge is getting the feel and the proper release point. One technique that is effective in getting the right release, especially in ensuring the pitch is thrown down in the zone, is to lengthen the stride slightly. This brings the release point lower and may also slow the pitch a bit.

There are only really two locations for this pitch—low and away (on the corner) and low and away (outside the strikezone). This applies equally to right- and left-handed batters. The pitch can be effective, if properly set up, from the middle to the outside half of the plate, down in the zone. If properly set up, it does not have to be thrown for a called strike. We are, after all, trying to fool the batter into swinging at a pitch he thinks is a fastball for a strike.

## Splitter

The split-finger fastball is thrown by inserting the ball between the index and middle fingers (Figure 14). Rather than being thrown with backspin (fastball), the ball comes out with little or no backspin. Rather, it tends to tumble with some forward spin. However, since it is thrown with fastball motion, it tends to have above average velocity. But, it tends to sink due to its tumbling action. It, therefore, looks like a fastball at release, but instead of "hopping" like a fastball, the bottom seems to fall out of it.

Figure 14. Splitter

The effectiveness of this pitch is based on the pitcher's ability to grip the ball properly, throw the pitch with velocity and control, and get the tumbling action necessary to get the pitch to sink. The amount that the fingers are split also affects velocity and the amount the ball tumbles. When thrown properly, it can be very effective down in the zone, especially as an out pitch (strikeout or ground out).

# SITUATIONAL PITCHING

> - Make him swing and miss.
> - Cause him to make a bad swing.
> - Force him to make a bad decision.
>
> Table 4. How to fool a hitter

Assuming that for most pitchers, the most effective method of beating the hitter is by fooling him, there are several considerations to take into account. There are three ways to fool the hitter, shown in Table 4. We can (a) make the batter swing and miss, with a combination of movement, speed, and location. (b) We can get him to make a bad swing, by forcing him to alter his mechanics in order to compensate for the actual pitch as compared with what he expected. And, (c) we can cause the hitter to make a bad decision—take a strike or chase a ball out of the zone.

Let me at this point acknowledge that there are many different philosophies regarding such concepts as "fooling the hitter," "going after the hitter," "nibbling," "being aggressive," and so on. On the one hand, we have been talking about the many weapons the pitcher has in his arsenal to cause the batter to make a mistake. We consider those mistakes what is listed in Table 4, which is a simplified list of the outcomes in Table 1 that are victories for the pitcher. Part of this discussion is about using those weapons (changing speeds, different movement, sequential pitching, and so on). Another part is location, and often this might mean throwing other than a strike. This aspect of situational pitching very much gets into the philosophy that any coach or team or organization has for its pitchers. So, the distinction here often centers around the notion of throwing pitches out of the strikezone, or just out of the strikezone; in contrast with being aggressive and throwing pitches in the strikezone. Some view the former as "nibbling," which can lead to throwing lots of pitches and losing a few hitters. The opposite is staying aggressive, throwing strikes, challenging hitters, and having confidence that the pitcher holds the advantage and that the probabilities favor the pitcher, even with good hitters.

Many major league organizations discourage an over-reliance on fooling hitters because they believe that philosophy leads to nibbling which leads to *aiming your pitches* which leads to many pitches and big innings. Instead, they teach young professional pitchers to worry less about fooling the hitter and more about making quality pitches down in the zone to induce contact. They want their pitchers to have the confidence that "their best" is always better than the hitter's best. Take that mindset, and success follows.

To me, there is no right answer. As in everything else, it depends. That is why we call it situational pitching. I do believe there are two imperatives that guide our strategy and tactics on the mound, and these imperatives tend to pull the two extremes (nibbling versus challenging) together: (a) throw strikes and (b) do not get beaten foolishly when you own the advantage. How pitchers walk the fine line between the various ends of the spectrum is what I would call the art of pitching. And, where you fall at any point in time depends on what you have for stuff and control and what the situation is in the game.

But let me be clear. I do not equate *fooling hitters* with *nibbling*. Fooling hitters means using your tools to win the battle (Table 5). That can be done while striving to throw all pitches for strikes. There is a difference to me in throwing an occasional pitch off the plate on the one hand, and on the other hand working on the edge or slightly out of the strikezone as a habit. The latter I would call nibbling and unless you have near-perfect command, is probably not a great idea.

- Location
- Movement
- Velocity
- Pitch selection and sequence

Table 5. Pitcher's tools (in order of importance)

So, assuming we want to challenge hitters, while fooling them at the same time, the pitcher has at his disposal at least four tools, listed in Table 5. He can vary the speed of his pitches, hit various locations, get movement on the ball, and very the sequence (strategically). We have already discussed how to obtain movement. Velocity is a matter of sound mechanics, strength, conditioning, and inherent characteristics such as body build. We now turn to the matter of pitch selection and location.

We begin by enumerating the factors, shown in Table 6, that must be considered in pitch selection—that is, what defines the "situation." Some are obvious, some more subtle. But, depending on the level of play, all affect the mind game that is going on between pitcher and hitter.

Of these factors, the most obvious is the count. However, to truly set hitters up to be fooled, you need to take into account as many of the rest as possible.

Hitters' characteristics include right- versus left-handed, kind of swing, stance, location in the box, size, power, bat speed, location in the lineup. Some of this information is obtained through scouting. Some is derived by observation. Catchers must become skilled at "reading" hitters, knowing the effect of certain stances and swing characteristics.

- Pitcher's Characteristics
- Game Situation
- Previous Results
- Hitter's Characteristics
- Count
- Weather
- Umpire

Table 6. Situational factors (in order of importance)

Pitchers should have a good feel for the capabilities and general traits of hitters in various places in the lineup. Table 7 summarizes some of the general characteristics of hitters through the lineup.

Pitchers' characteristics are fairly obvious, but they need to be compared to the hitter. For example, a power pitcher throws differently to a power hitter from the way a finesse pitcher throws to the same hitter.

Game situation includes the outs, the score, baserunners, inning, and so on. Previous result refers to how we pitched to the batter in his last at bat, the at bat before that, and previous encounters. One effective way to account for previous result is by charting pitches, and saving those charts from game to game. Nothing is more helpful than to know, "What did we throw this guy last time, and what was the result?" In addition, pitchers, catchers, and pitching coaches should review hitters before games, and between innings.

Two other considerations include the umpire and the weather. The strikezone any given day is the strikezone the umpire is calling, *not the one in the rule book*. Pitchers need to throw to that zone and take advantage where possible (low strike, corners). Most importantly, pitchers need to avoid becoming frustrated, especially visually, with an umpire's strikezone. Just consider that the zone is what he is calling, and nothing else. If you get squeezed, you may have to rely more on pitch selection and change of speed than location.

Weather can also influence pitches. Recall our discussion of how air affects pitches. On hot days we can expect better velocity and less movement. The ball will also carry better. Winds exert a significant effect. Tail winds increase velocity and decrease movement. Head winds increase movement and decrease velocity. Cross winds can affect lateral movement. Cold weather can make the ball more slippery, requiring the pitcher to find some moisture (legally) to enhance the grip. Rain can make the ball heavier and more slippery. The time to work out adjustments is during warm up. (See the section on the mental aspects of pitching.) Enter the game with an idea of what likely will work and what won't. Fold this in with a good analysis of the hitters to form a game plan.

Ask most pitchers what is the factor they first consider in pitch selection and they will respond with count. Table 8 provides some general rules of thumb for pitch selection based on count.

| Location in Lineup | Traits | Remarks |
|---|---|---|
| 1, 2 | · contact hitter not easily fooled<br>· good eye for strikezone & strikes out rarely<br>· good bunter<br>· good bat control<br>· good hitter for average, minimal power | · can be overpowered<br>· no need to nibble<br>· don't expect to chase balls |
| 3 | · best overall hitter – average & power<br>· will hurt you on mistakes<br>· can hurt you on good pitches<br>· generally great fastball hitters<br>· can hit anything in zone | · more susceptible to breaking pitches & offspeed than fastballs<br>· find weakness<br>· avoid fastballs on heart<br>· cannot be overpowered<br>· cannot get away with balls on inner ½ of plate |
| 4 | · best power hitter in lineup<br>· fastball hitter<br>· less foot speed than 1, 2, & 3<br>· may chase out of zone<br>· big swing | · susceptible to offspeed<br>· avoid heart of zone<br>· avoid out over plate at medium height where he likes to extend arms<br>· miss way in or low and away |
| 5, 6 | · similar to 4 but less capable | · see 4 |
| 7, 8 | · *relatively* weakest hitters in lineup<br>· may have speed<br>· limited power | · can be overpowered<br>· may be fooled<br>· watch giving in with offspeed if he cannot handle fastball |
| 9 | · relatively weak hitter<br>· may have traits of leadoff hitter (including speed, bunting ability) | · see 7, 8 |

Table 7. Characteristics of hitters through the lineup

Pitchers must be cautious of becoming predictable, especially in relation to pitch selection in certain counts. Therefore, though there are certainly high probability of success spots in certain counts, other considerations may dictate other pitch locations. These factors we have talked about, but predominantly include what has happened on previous at bats, the game situation, and how the batter has been set up on this at bat. Nevertheless, there are some basic rules of thumb for how to pitch at each count.

| Count | Remarks |
|---|---|
| 0-0 | get a strike w/ any pitch that be thrown with confidence |
| 0-1 | make him chase marginal strike |
| 0-2 / 1-2 | make him chase out of zone |
| 1-1 | get another strike not necessarily grooved |
| 2-2 | best pitch available for a strike |
| 3-2 | throw a strike w/ any pitch thrown with confidence |
| behind | get a strike<br>offspeed is good choice if control is good |

Table 8. Pitches by count

Let's consider the walk. There are times when walking a batter may be a good outcome. This gets back to my earlier discussion of pitching philosophy. But, (and not everyone will agree) here is one view about the circumstances in which a walk might be acceptable:

- Pitching carefully to a good hitter in certain situations.
- An open base.
- To set up a double-play.

We know that there are three ways to walk a hitter, the first of which is not acceptable and that is simply lacking control. Nothing much good comes from unintentional walks. It puts a runner on who did not earn the base. Fielders get complacent. And it is emotionally defeating to everyone. Finally, it puts you in the stretch.

But, the second way we can walk a hitter is when we work a hitter carefully and accept a walk if he does not bite on pitches out of the zone, when we would rather not get hurt in a critical situation—the "intentional-unintentional walk." And, of course, there is the intentional walk.

## Locations by Count

Figure 15 depicts the strikezone (the patterned square starting 22" above the plate), as measured at the front of the plate.

Remember, however, that the ball will drop several inches more from the front of the plate to the catcher's glove. Assuming the catcher's glove is 3 to 4 feet behind the front of the plate, a pitch will drop an additional 4 inches (90 mph) to 10 inches (65 mph). What this obviously means is the target must be set lower ( ▪ ).

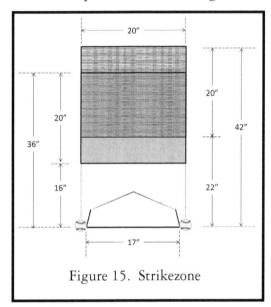

Figure 15. Strikezone

We can now look at some general rules of thumb for location based on count. We start by depicting the strikezone as a set of smaller "zones" where we might set up a target (see Figure 16). Note that there is a small portion of the strikezone, at the top, that umpires may or may not call strikes, which is called the "high strike." This is heavily dependent on the individual ump.

Note that there are zones on either half of the plate, zones on the corners (strikes), and zones clearly off the plate (out of the strikezone). Depending on count, as shown in Table 8, we may or may not be trying to throw a strike. The essence of control is *not* throwing strikes, but rather *hitting spots*. For example, unless the pitcher is completely overpowering or without control, we might choose to set up outside the strikezone on an 0-2 count.

Within the vertical confines of the strikezone, we can also identify zones that are high, medium, and low, in addition to zones below the strikezone.

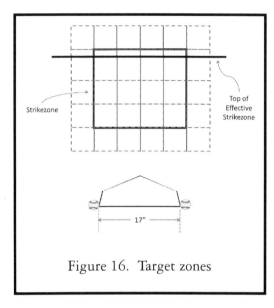

Figure 16. Target zones

With that in mind, we can begin to identify some rules of thumb based on count. The figures are predicated on a right-hand batter. Again, it must be stressed that the real-time situation may dictate another target location.

These zones can be used with any pitch. When it is important to throw a strike, pitch selection should take into account what the pitcher has going for him on that day, and what he has a high confidence of throwing for a strike.

Keep in mind, also, that the catcher's target should be placed so that the ball passes through the strikezone at the front of the plate. The figures, therefore, show generalized zones where the pitch should be thrown, and where the catcher should set his target.

On the first pitch (Figure 17) we see that the general objective is to throw a strike. Depending on the pitcher's control, we can target the corners. Secondarily, we can target the outside half of the plate, but (depending on the batter) avoid a fat

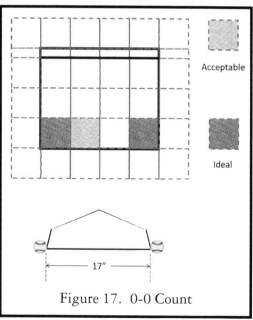

Figure 17. 0-0 Count

pitch on the inside half of the plate. Obviously, considerable judgment must apply, and the specific zones must be tailored to the pitcher, the opponent, the team, and the coach's pitching philosophies.

For the 0-1 count (Figure 18), we still want to throw a strike, but don't need to groove it. We also can bust the hitter inside, depending on where the 0-0 pitch was thrown.

With two strikes, there are at last two tactics (as discussed before), and these depend on (a) the pitcher's stuff and command and (b) the situation, and (c) the team's philosophy. In one tactic (philosophy), we want to get the hitter to chase a ball out of the zone. Good choices include low and away, low and in, up and in, and high heat out of the zone (depending on the pitcher's velocity and movement). I believe there is absolutely no excuse for getting hurt 0-2. Therefore, I want the hitter to chase a bad pitch. The choice of pitch depends heavily on what's been thrown already, and what the gameplan is for the next, "out" pitch (Figure 19).

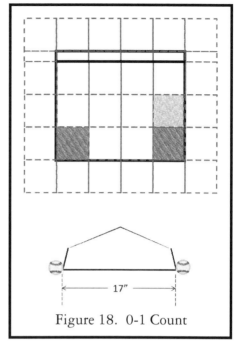

Figure 18. 0-1 Count

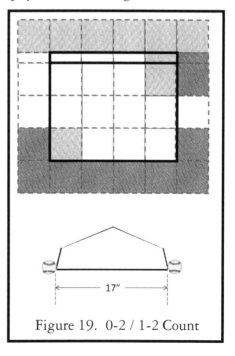

Figure 19. 0-2 / 1-2 Count

Of course, the other tactic is to go after the hitter with your best. If a pitcher has overwhelming stuff, is ahead in the game, facing a hitter late in the lineup, and/or considering previous at bats, the pitcher may simply challenge the hitter and beat him with a good pitch in the zone. This is a bet: a .300 hitter will succeed less than 1/3 of the time, generally. And, again, this philosophy tries to avoid the tendency to nibble or to squander the advantage. So, challenge the hitter.
I think it depends!

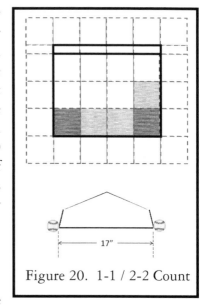

Figure 20. 1-1 / 2-2 Count

On a 1-1 or 2-2 count (Figure 20), we want another strike, but would rather not groove the pitch depending on the pitcher's control. In fact, for a pitcher with excellent control, the 2-2 count target can revert to the 0-2/1-2 count.

On a 3-2 count, we want a strike with any pitch the pitcher has confidence in. The only difference from the 2-2 count is that we are more inclined to throw a more grooved strike, to avoid walking the hitter (Figure 21).

All in all, we would like to avoid the 3-2 count. In fact, we'd prefer to avoid any 3 ball count. Our goal is to never get past 2-2—get the hitter at 2-2. If behind in the count, obviously try to get ahead—back to 2 strikes—or get the hitter to hit into an out.

So, if behind, we need to get a strike, with any pitch we have confidence in. With control over pitches other than fastballs, we can go to offspeed when

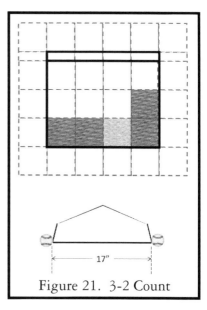

Figure 21. 3-2 Count

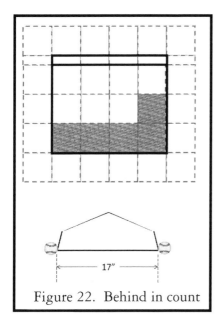

Figure 22. Behind in count

behind in the count, hoping to fool a batter looking fastball (Figure 22). Obviously, the key in all of this is control—the ability to hit spots, preferably with every pitch in the arsenal. That allows us to get ahead, stay ahead, get the batter to chase something undesirable, and to get back even when we fall behind.

## Setting Up Hitters

The essence of fooling hitters is mastering the art of setting them up. That is, what we want the hitter to do is expect one pitch, get another, then realize too late to adjust. This keeps him from teeing off on "his" pitch. If early in the count, he gets something unexpected. With two strikes, he must protect the plate. So, we want to make him protect by chasing something essentially unhittable. In every case, we want him to either swing at something he cannot hit, or is weak at hitting; or, let a called strike go by. There are several ways to do this.

1. The first step is to know where each hitter is weak—that is, where his weak zones are—and where his strong zones are, so we can throw to the weak zones, and avoid the strong zones. But, be careful to avoid the tendency to stray from your own strengths just because they are the hitter's strengths as well. Have confidence in your own abilities.

2. Have a plan to expand the size of his weak zones. This means, extending the weak parts of his strikezone to include areas out of the strikezone where he is forced to protect by virtue of the pitcher getting ahead in the count, especially two strikes.

3. Vary the pitching pattern on successive at bats. Avoid getting into a predictable pattern. For example, one at bat you might get a hitter

to chase the low and away breaking ball. Next time up, get two strikes and bust him up and in with a fastball.

4. Get ahead in the count, then make the hitter chase a ball out of the zone where he feels the need to protect, and where the pitcher has little risk of falling too far behind. Again, unless the pitcher is overpowering relative to the hitter, there is no reason to throw a *hittable* strike with an 0-2 and, depending on control, a 1-2 count.

5. Change speeds. Table 9 shows how many feet less an offspeed pitch travels in the same time it takes for a fastball to reach the front of the plate. For example, compared to an 85 mph fastball, a 75 mph offspeed pitch will be 6 feet farther in front of the plate in the same time the fastball would have taken to reach the front of the plate. In other words, if the batter swings at what he thinks is an 85 mph fastball, when the pitch is actually traveling at 75 mph, he will be 6 feet out in front. What this tells you is you do not have to change speed much for the batter to be ahead or behind the ball. The closer the speed between the fastball and the offspeed, the tougher the difference is to detect. Of course, the batter will swing at the pitch thrown. If the speeds are close, he might be able to adjust. So, there is some tradeoff between being able to fool the batter into thinking he is seeing a fastball, and having enough of a difference in the speeds for the batter to miss significantly. Incidentally, Table 10 provides the differential speeds for major league pitchers during the 2012 season (according to www.fangraphs.com) in order of decreasing speed.

6. Here are a few observations from Table 10. Note the average differences in pitch velocity (and, the percentage speed of each pitch). For example, the average major league changeup takes 7.8 mph off the fastball (not altogether different from the speed differential of sliders). Note that cutters and splitters are thrown relatively hard (roughly 93 to 96% of fastball velocity). Curveballs average about 14 mph slower than fastballs. The point here is that we can see what velocity major league pitches are compared to fastballs, and use these not to see how hard to throw, but what kind of differential might be appropriate (in terms of speed difference or percentage of fastball speed).

7. Throw what the batter is not expecting. This has to do with deciding on a sequence of pitches purposely designed to get the hitter to expect one pitch and get another. To do this effectively requires thinking back to previous at bats, as well as thinking about

| Difference in Feet Traveled | | Velocity of Offspeed Pitch | | | | | |
|---|---|---|---|---|---|---|---|
| | | 90 | 85 | 80 | 75 | 70 | 65 | 60 |
| Velocity of Fastball | 95 | 2.8 | 5.7 | 8.5 | 11.4 | 14.2 | 17.1 | 19.9 |
| | 90 | ---- | 3.0 | 6.0 | 9.0 | 12.0 | 15.0 | 18.0 |
| | 85 | ---- | ---- | 3.2 | 6.4 | 9.5 | 12.7 | 15.9 |
| | 80 | ---- | ---- | ---- | 3.4 | 6.7 | 10.1 | 13.5 |
| | 75 | ---- | ---- | ---- | ---- | 3.6 | 7.2 | 10.8 |
| | 70 | ---- | ---- | ---- | ---- | ---- | 3.9 | 7.7 |
| | 65 | ---- | ---- | ---- | ---- | ---- | ---- | 4.2 |

Table 9. Difference in feet traveled

| | | Fastball | Cutter | Splitter | Slider | Changeup | Curveball |
|---|---|---|---|---|---|---|---|
| Average Speed by Pitch | Average | 91.1 | 87.8 | 84.5 | 83.5 | 83.2 | 76.8 |
| | Highest | 95.5 | 92.6 | 87.7 | 87.5 | 88.7 | 83.1 |
| | Lowest | 83.4 | 82.9 | 80.8 | 76.1 | 75.0 | 71.2 |
| Average Difference from Fastball | Average Difference | NA | -3.1 | -6.9 | -7.6 | -7.8 | -14.3 |
| | % of Fastball | | 96.4% | 92.7% | 91.6% | 91.4% | 84.4% |
| | Highest Avg Difference | | -6.2 | -9.2 | -13.0 | -11.9 | -19.6 |
| | Lowest Avg Difference | | +0.2 | -5.0 | -3.6 | -3.4 | -8.0 |

Table 10. Difference in speed from fastball

the pitches and results during the current at bat. For example, you might work the outside corner with a couple of pitches, then bust the hitter in on the fists. Or conversely, throw him a fastball up and in with two strikes, then follow up with offspeed low and away for the out pitch. These are simple examples, but they illustrate the idea. The concept can be as detailed as desired. For example, on successive at bats, you need to think about what you threw before, and vary it, depending on results. If successful, the batter may expect to see the same thing—so change it. If unsuccessful, the batter may not expect you to use it again. The choice here depends on how the pitcher feels about the pitch.

8. Vary movement. For pitchers adept at using movement, they can alternate between sinkers and cut fastballs. Alternate between 2- and 4-seam fastballs. Any movement, if controlled, is effective at creating miss distance for the batter.

9. Disguise your pitches. The simplest form of this idea is to ensure every pitch has similar arm motion, so that offspeed pitches look like fastballs. We do not want to tip our pitches with obvious or subtle changes that can distinguish one pitch from another.

10. Use motion to fool the hitter. Some pitchers subtly increase the speed of their windup on offspeed, or slow down their windup on fastballs.

11. Work the extremes of the strikezone: up and in, down and out. In other words, work the batter off the plate, then go after the outside corner. Get him leaning over the plate, bust him in on the hands. Change the *look angle* for the hitter.

12. Ahead in the count, use high heat. Often a fastball high in the zone looks attractive, but is much tougher to hit than it seems. This is especially true inside, particularly with movement up and in. To hit high heat, especially in, requires the hitter to get the bat started early and generate a lot of bat speed to get the head of the bat out in front of the plate in order to make contact with the ball.

13. Throw offspeed and breaking pitches low in the zone, generally away. They often look like strikes part way to the plate, only to die in the dirt behind the plate. Hopefully, the batter commits early and can't hold up on a ball that is really out of the zone low.

14. Start breaking pitches on the outside part of the plate so they break out of the strikezone where they cannot be hit hard. Against left-

handed hitters, start sinkers on the outside to break out of the zone away. Similarly, try to catch the outside corner with a breaking ball that starts and looks outside. Don't miss over the plate, though. Keep in mind, however, that good hitters can recognize these pitches and take them, unless you have set them up. Thus, the importance of having a plan for your sequence of pitches.

15. Have more than one speed on the fastball. No need to throw it as hard as possible every pitch (100%). Rather, throw the fastball at something less than full out most of the time. You can load up when you need a little extra velocity, and back off for an effective offspeed pitch.

16. Finally, never forget the benefits of throwing strikes (staying ahead in the count and "pitching to contact") and relying on your defense as an important weapon in your arsenal.

In summary, to fool hitters you need to throw what they're not expecting. That means *in* when they expect *away*, *up* when they are looking *down*, *offspeed* when they expect *heat*, *heat* when they are guessing *offspeed*, and *movement* other than what they are looking for. This requires planning ahead and thinking on the mound. This is the essence of sequential pitching, having a game plan, considering all facets of the situation and what has already happened, and executing good pitching tactics. Remember that seeing enough of the same pitch, every hitter has the potential to hit it hard. So, we need to be either overpowering or unpredictable or both.

# WARMING UP TO PITCH A GAME

There are several reasons why we warm up before pitching in a game:

1. The obvious—to warm up the arm and body to pitch.
2. To gain confidence with every pitch.
3. To find out what kind of stuff we've got that day—velocity, movement, control.
4. To get a feel for the conditions—wind, moisture, temperature.
5. To make any adjustments to mechanics.

Be precise as to the time before game time you start to warm up, depending on whether you are home or away. Done properly, warm up should take about 20 minutes

Begin with a light run around the park, to get the blood flowing. Do some stretching. A good number of pitching-style stretching exercises can be found in some of Tom House's books.

Be aware of the configuration of the bullpen. Is the direction the same, or roughly the same as the mound on the playing field? If not, be aware that the wind conditions will alter the ball differently from warming up to the game. Is the mound the same size or shape as the real thing? Is the bullpen mound properly maintained, or is the pivot hole dug out? If possible, you can maintain your own bullpen in preparation for pitching a game. In short, be aware of the similarities and differences between the mounds in the pen and on the field.

Before entering the pen, begin some light throwing, at about 45 feet. On each pitch, extend the arm further. Increase the distance quickly and gradually, until you are throwing from about 90 feet—not hard, but with a long arm motion. Why long toss before warming up? This very effectively stretches out the arm while forcing the pitcher to hit small targets from long distance. After a few throws at 90 feet, move into the pen and begin to warm up on the mound.

Begin throwing fastballs, increasing velocity to your best and throw eight. Then start with easy breaking balls, increasing to your hardest breaking ball. Throw some change-ups, then begin mixing up all your pitches as in a game. Throw some from the stretch, both the full stretch and the glide step.

Stop after throwing for a total of 10-15 minutes.

# CORRECTING PROBLEMS

When control starts to wander, there are several considerations. If the misses are consistent, that points to a specific mechanical problem. For example, missing left for a righthanded pitcher means he is most likely opening up with the front shoulder too soon. Pitcher needs to focus on driving his front shoulder and chin toward the target, striding down the line toward the target, with the idea of driving all momentum toward the target.

Missing right and low is often caused by stepping right of the line, and throwing across the body (loss of velocity) or missing low and left. Missing high and right is probably just an early release, often as the result of an incomplete follow-through. Watch for the pitcher's posture following release. He is probably standing erect, with the arm never finishing low and left. This is also reason for concern as the rapid deceleration of the arm will eventually take its toll. This problem is especially noticeable on off-speed pitches hung or otherwise thrown high.

Erratic loss of control is tougher to pinpoint. Often, the flow from rocker step to release has gotten out of sequence—the arm either rushing through ahead of the body, or lagging the body. One simple solution, especially during practice and in the pen, is to ask the pitcher to very slightly pause in the "stork" position. This tends to anchor the whole motion, get it back into a proper sequence, and allow the arm and stride to occur with a comfortable and smooth flow.

Erratic control is the result of an inconsistent release. Just like a golf swing, the idea is to be able to repeat the motion consistently. So, if the release is changing pitch to pitch, then something in the mechanics is changing on each pitch. Look for the big keys first: tendency to lean during various parts of the windup; head, eyes, and shoulders not level; hand not on top of the ball in the extended position; throwing arm pointing left or right of 2B when extended; inconsistent arm motion (varying from overhand to ¾); and so on.

With breaking pitches, the problem is most often hanging it high, or missing low and left. Hanging the pitch high is often the result of an incomplete follow-through or a failure to pull the pitch down hard in front of you. Another possible solution is to have the pitcher extend the stride slightly. Missing low and left is caused by premature opening up of the left shoulder. Have the pitcher focus on driving the chin and left shoulder toward the target.

With change-ups, when the pitcher leaves it high consistently, the release is too high. Either correct the early release, or have him slightly extend his stride. Better to miss low than high.

# MENTAL ASPECTS OF PITCHING

Here is a list of the various considerations that impact the mental aspects of pitching. Thus far, we have covered a bit of the physics of pitching, the strategy and tactics, and some other aspects of being a competent hurler. But, pitching is a complex endeavor, and there are many aspects of pitching that impact success on the hill. Here are some of them:

*Cognitive*: the cognitive aspects of pitching are what we covered in the preceding pages.

*Emotional*: being capable of controlling emotions and channeling them toward successful outcomes is essential. Here is a list of some of the emotional attributes (attitude) that describe excellent pitchers:

- Toughness
- Resiliency
- Memory (or, a lack of memory when that serves you); so, perhaps Selective Memory
- Courage
- Confidence
- Honesty (as contrasted with the other attributes, especially when tired, hurt, or not your best)

*More Attitude-related Attributes:*

- Willingness to prepare (physically and mentally—game plans)
- Self-evaluation: the ability to self-critique AND to be willing to take criticism
- Relationships founded on trust and communication, especially with your catcher and your pitching coach.
- "Resetting": the ability to use some mental trick or breathing or physical mechanism to wipe away some negative outcome over which you no longer have control, and then to focus on successfully executing the next pitch.

*Other Abilities that Contribute to Success* (or, "Helping Yourself Out"):

- Fielding your position (grounders, pops, bunts, right-side grounders, covering bases)
- Backing up bases on hits
- Communication with fielders
- Holding runners
- Pickoffs
- Hitting and bunting
- Hydration
- Coping with cooling off and long innings
- Charting and interpreting charts of pitches
- Warming up properly
- Knowing, interpreting, and communicating how you feel and what you have that day
- Signs

## About Mechanics

One important consideration regarding the mental aspects of pitching is worthy of some discussion. We tend to dwell on mechanics, especially with young pitchers, and often during a game when there is a mechanical flaw leading to inconsistent deliveries and poor control. The danger in this is getting a pitcher too focused on the mechanics of the delivery during a game. In this situation, there are far mort important things to occupy a pitcher's mind; and, perhaps far more better ways to approach the mental challenge of throwing quality pitches. Moreover, a preoccupation with mechanics is most likely to have more negative effects than positive ones.

An appropriate analogy here is with the game of golf. Pitching and golf are very similar in terms of the physical and some of the mental aspects.

Dr. Bob Rotella is widely considered to be the world's preeminent sports psychologist and performance coach. His books (in particular, *Golf is Not a Game of Perfect* and *The Golfer's Mind*) are as relevant to baseball as they are to golf. Any pitcher who wants to master the mental aspects of his craft, and any coach who aspires to understand the mental aspects of pitching, should read these books and the other teachings of Bob Rotella.

In a nutshell, his theme is that successful golf is mostly about conquering the mental aspects of the golf swing and strategy. Mastering the mechanics is important, for no one can succeed without a basically sound set of fundamentals. But, this is accomplished through practice and not an appropriate nor effective focus during a game. In a game situation, the most successful approach is distinctly devoid of a fixation or concern with mechanics. Rather, the most successful approach is to have a positive outlook, a success-oriented attitude, visualizing the desired shape and result of pitches, and relying on the mechanical habits learned through repetition during practice.

Baseball, particularly pitching, is as Dr. Rotella described golf, "a game of confidence and competence." Dr. Rotella cautioned that he does claim "that a player who lacks physical skills can transform overnight into a winner by changing his thinking. If you trust [bad mechanics], it's still going to produce bad [pitches]. (Though it will produce fewer of them than if you don't trust it.) You have to attain a level of physical competence to play well." But, Dr. Rotella explained that "it's impossible to overestimate the importance of the mind . . . . There is no such thing as 'muscle memory.' Your muscles have no capacity to remember anything. Memory resides in your head. Therefore, no matter how long you practice [pitching], no matter how skilled you become, your muscles alone can't remember it and execute it when the need arises . . . . Your muscles and the rest of your body are controlled by your mind. Unless your mind is functioning well when you [pitch], your muscles are going to flounder. If your head is filled with bad thoughts, your [performance] is going to be full of bad [pitches]."

In his many articles in *Golf Digest*, Dr. Rotella provided several principles and keys that lead to a successful golf swing. These are equally applicable to pitching. Here are a few of Dr. Rotella's principles, mostly in his words with slight alterations for pitching. These I offer as a good starting point for mastering the mental aspects of pitching.

1. "Believe you can win." Simply put, go out to the hill with confidence.

2. "Don't be seduced by results." It's called staying in the present, not allowing yourself to be seduced by a score or by winning. Get lost in the process of executing each pitch and accept the result. The process is, for the most part, the following: (a) Have a game plan and a plan for each hitter. (b) Select a pitch and a location. (c) Pick a target. (d) Visualize the pitch. (e) Execute the pitch.

3. "Sulking won't get you anything. The worst thing you can do for your prospects of winning is to get down when things don't go well. If you start feeling sorry for yourself or thinking the . . . gods are conspiring against you, you're not focused on the next [pitch]."

4. "Ignore unsolicited . . . advice." Mostly, avoid having mechanical thoughts or making changes during a game, unless there is an

obvious and easily corrected flaw you can eliminate. The only advice you should trust is from your catcher and pitching coach. As Dr. Rotella stated, "You'll have lots of well-meaning friends who want to give you advice. Don't accept it. In fact, stop them before they can say a word. Their comments will creep into your mind when you're on the [mound]. If you've worked on your game, commit to the plan and stay confident."

5. "Have a routine to lean on." Have and follow "mental and physical routine on every [pitch]. It keeps you focused on what you have to do, and when the pressure is on, it helps you manage your nerves."

6. "Find peace on the [mound]. When you practice hard and admit to yourself that you really want to win, it's easy to build up a [game] into something so huge that you can't play. . . . The [mound] has to be your sanctuary, the thing you love, and you can't be afraid of messing up."

7. "Play to play great. Don't play not to play poorly. . . . Players who play to play great understand that good can be the enemy of great. They know that if they get too concerned about not being bad, they might not free themselves up enough to be great. . . . They play to win."

8. "Love the challenge of the day, whatever it may be." Every day is different: different conditions, different opponent, different abilities you bring to the hill, different teammate performance, different umpires. The key is "reacting well to inevitable mistakes and misfortunes." You will never have complete control of the game, but you can control your attitude. Dr. Rotella spoke of "anger and frustration as impediments to playing the game as well as you can. For starters, if you're angry, you're not focused . . . . On top of that, anger introduces tension into the body. Tension damages rhythm and grace. It hinders your effort to get your mind and body into the state where you play your best. . . . Accept whatever happens . . . and move on."

9. "Believe fully in yourself so you can play freely." Dr. Rotella defines confidence in golf terms as follows: "Confident golfers think about what they want to happen on the course. Golfers who lack confidence think about the things they don't want to happen. That's all confidence is. It's not arrogance. It's not experience. It's simply thinking about the things you want to happen on the golf course." This is directly applicable to pitching.

10. "Be decisive, committed and clear. Trust is a must.... We want as much as possible to govern our bodies with our subconscious mind. That's because, in sport, the human body works most effectively when the conscious mind is shut off. Call it instinct, or intuition or the right side of the brain if you're more comfortable with those concepts than you are with the notion of the subconscious. Whatever you call it, you want it in control when you [pitch]. You ... must trust your [delivery], you must believe that it will work.

# PITCHING MECHANICS: A CHECKLIST

So, now that we have established the proper relationship between mechanics and the mental aspects of pitching, let's talk mechanics. Since there are so many books on pitching mechanics, I instead have provided a checklist of specific mechanical points to look at when addressing the mechanics of individual pitchers. There is a tradeoff, like many sports, between basic, well accepted fundamentals and individual style. The following is meant to be more a collection of areas to look at, with a few "opinions."

## GENERAL

- ☐ Styles (very individual):
    - o Power – exceptional velocity, stuff, and control
    - o Control – the rest of us
- ☐ Most common flaw – overthrowing to achieve velocity
- ☐ 3 most important tools for the successful pitcher:
    - o Control
    - o Movement
    - o Velocity
- ☐ Grip: 4-seam for control, 2-seam for movement
- ☐ Mechanical checkpoints:

- - Draw line straight from stance on rubber toward target
  - Note where stride foot lands
  - Adjust based on release, location of pitch – tradeoff between throwing across body and opening up to soon
  - Learn to make corrections to adjust for mechanical problems
  - Go back to basic mechanics when out of rhythm
- Movement achieved by:
  - Grip
  - Wrist
  - Thumb
  - Pressure on first two fingers
- Breathing

## STANCE

- Right (pivot) foot on right side of rubber (RH) and opposite for LH
- Left foot slightly aft and left (45 degrees)
- Most of weight on pivot foot
- Take sign on rubber while concealing ball (in glove or behind back)

## ROCKER STEP

- 45" transfer step
- Short—to avoid rushing body ahead of arm
- Weight remains balanced—merely taking some weight off pivot foot to easily turn it
- Avoid extremes—not straight back, not sideways--45" works

well because it cuts down on total amount of body movement to get to good "stork" position
- ☐ Keep shoulders "in" the strikezone—pointed toward target andnot leaned back
- ☐ Joint hands at waist
- ☐ Raise hands and transfer weight to left foot

## PIVOT

- ☐ Turn pivot foot perpendicular to the line to the plate—parallel to rubber
- ☐ Place pivot foot properly onto front of rubber—can even look down momentarily to ensure foot in desired spot
- ☐ Slight flex in front knee, but don't drop down too far
- ☐ As soon as pivot foot in place, look back up to lock-on to target

## LIFT AND LOAD—THE "STORK" POSITION

- ☐ Shift weight forward to pivot foot
- ☐ Pick up left foot from the knee down (not the hip) with a relaxed front foot
- ☐ Lift leg so knee is slightly above waist—thigh is at least parallel to ground
- ☐ Turn body toward 3B (for RH)
- ☐ Remain balanced—avoid tendency to lean back either toward 1B or 2B
- ☐ Able to balance on pivot foot and hold it forever
- ☐ Locked on to target
- ☐ Knees aligned--110° turn away from plate
- ☐ Point butt at plate—hips and shoulders have turned past the

plate
- [ ] In a cocked, spring-like position—stored energy
- [ ] Some but not excessive flex in back leg
- [ ] Hands remain high in front of chest with ball concealed from batter

## Unload and Begin Stride

- [ ] Slight but noticeable increase in the flex/bend of the right knee
- [ ] Weight on the inside ball of the pivot foot
- [ ] Start to glide forward
- [ ] Avoid tendency to rush, especially the upper body—keep lead shoulder "closed"—pointed at target until the last possible moment
- [ ] Avoid tendency to open up too fast with the upper body and lead shoulder—causes loss of velocity and tendency to miss left, especially with breaking ball

## Stride into the Power Position

- [ ] Hands move down toward raised bend leg and separate before touching lifted leg
- [ ] Early break of the hands to begin large arm circle with throwing arm
- [ ] Break hands and extend arms, like "breaking an egg over front leg" with thumbs going downward the outward away from each other
  - Late hands break—hurts power, tendency to miss high
  - Early break allows getting arm back early and through more quickly without rushing

- ☐ Avoid tendency (especially among infielders) to short arm—no big arm circle with throwing arm
  - o Caused by late break of hands
  - o A shortcut to get arm through
- ☐ Glove hand extends toward target with glove opening toward 1B
- ☐ Ball hand extends toward 2B with fingers on top of ball
- ☐ Elbows and knees flexed
- ☐ Definitely locked on to target
- ☐ Body still closed toward 3B
- ☐ Head and eyes level
- ☐ Raised front leg swings toward target in straight line gaining momentum
- ☐ Gliding forward in linear motion toward target

## Dynamic Energy Change

- ☐ Left foot opens up and lands slightly to left of stride line
- ☐ Land toe-to-heel, relaxed
  (landing on heel tends to lock front leg)
- ☐ Long stride—body low to ground—back knee can be close to touching ground
- ☐ Backside pushes front side out as front arm pulls in toward side of body
- ☐ Elbow pulled down obliquely and glove hand is pulled in to chest to start and accelerate upper body rotation
- ☐ Think "stride and late rotate" to keep shoulder closed for as long as possible and gain most rotation possible
- ☐ Throwing arm abeam head as left foot lands, completing large arm circle

- ☐ Upper body opening up, transferring linear motion to rotary force—taking momentum toward plate and transferring it to a rotation
- ☐ Inward rotation of back knee now driving back foot off the rubber
- ☐ Chest over front leg—ahead of waist—pointing at plate—moving toward catcher
- ☐ For more velocity, think quicker arm, not "muscling up"

## Explosive Release

- ☐ Back knee totally rotated toward plate
- ☐ Glove all the way pulled to chest
- ☐ Shoulders no longer level—slightly tilted away from throwing arm
- ☐ Elbow up by ear
- ☐ Ball is released out in front of head
- ☐ Throwing hand continues forward then down across chest ending 2" left of ankle
- ☐ Most of weight on left leg
- ☐ Bent over at waist
- ☐ Eyes still on target, continuous since first picked up

## Hip-Roll-and Follow-Through

- ☐ Hips and back leg come around into follow through
- ☐ Back foot comes up and over as result of powerful stride and release
- ☐ Avoid rapid deceleration of the arm following release--this action keeps stress off arm
- ☐ Head and neck bows up to keep eyes up and on target

# THE NINTH INNING: THE FINISH

Pitching is a complex endeavor—both physical and mental. While there are many views on how to succeed as a pitcher, in this book there are several principles that I believe lead to success on the mound. Among these are the following:

- There is no substitute for hard work at the physical aspects of pitching (conditioning, mechanics) during practice.
- Regarding the physical aspects of pitching, there is a limited number of things you can do with a ball: give it speed, give it direction, impart spin, and select an orientation of the seams. You can also combine pitches in different sequences and combinations. Otherwise, there is nothing you can do to the ball.
- Therefore, every other factor that you can control is mental.
- The mental aspects of pitching are far reaching, and absolutely essential to success. These can be grouped in two major categories:
    o    Preparation: the game plan
    o    In game: having confidence and visualizing good pitches.

- You cannot succeed consistently on the hill without having a plan in mind beforehand.
- Do not count on overpowering every hitter.
- But, realize that a great hitter fails 60-70% of the time.
- If you prepare well, then have confidence that you will win each battle with hitters.
- Be smart: to succeed at high levels of ball requires that you deliver the right pitch in the right spot and at the right time.
- Do not overreact to a failure. Sometimes, stuff happens. Move on and execute the next pitch.
- Walk the fine line between being aggressive and making smart pitches.

Your objective on the mound is getting outs, as efficiently as possible for as long as possible. There is a strategy to doing this and it relies upon a thoughtful approach that considers your abilities and the situation. If you combine great physical preparation with a sound mental approach, you greatly increase your chances to get those outs, succeed on the hill, and give your team the best opportunity to win games.

# ABOUT THE AUTHOR

Dr. Branford McAllister has been involved with baseball for over 50 years, as player, coach, fan, and student of the game. He was a right-handed pitcher for over 20 years as an amateur player at both NAIA and Division I college levels and in competitive amateur adult baseball leagues. He has coached at all levels from youth through high school. During his long baseball career he has been an astute student of the game, focusing on an in-depth and unique understanding of the science, art, and strategy of pitching.

Professionally, Dr. McAllister spent a full career in the US Air Force as a fighter pilot followed by his ongoing career as a weapon systems engineer. He has a bachelors degree in mathematics from the USAF Academy and graduate degrees in history, engineering administration, and management. He has a website (www.mcallister-associates.com) devoted to leadership and doctoral research.

Dr. McAllister lives in Niceville, Florida, with his wife of over 37 years, with whom he has two adult children he coached throughout their amateur sports careers.

This is his first book on baseball, and captures much of the knowledge gained over his many years of thinking about and teaching the craft of pitching.

Printed in Poland
by Amazon Fulfillment
Poland Sp. z o.o., Wrocław